W9-CCR-928

THE HOPIS

A First Americans Book

Virginia Driving Hawk Sneve

illustrated by Ronald Himler

Holiday House/New York

ACKNOWLEDGMENTS

The quotations of Percy Lomaquahu, Daisy Hooee, Tracy Kavena, and Dextra Quotskuyva are taken from *Talking with the Clay: The Art of Pueblo Pottery*, by Stephen Trimble (Santa Fe, NM: School of American Research Press, 1987). Copyright 1987 by Stephen Trimble. Reprinted by permission of Stephen Trimble.

The quotation of Al Qoyawayma is from *Al Qoyawayma: Hopi Potter* (Sante Fe, NM: Santa Fe East Gallery, 1984).

The quotation of Polingaysi Qoyawayma is from *No Turning Back: A Hopi Indian Woman's Struggle to Live in Two Worlds* (Albuquerque, NM: University of New Mexico Press, 1977).

The Hopi Elders' quotation is from *Handbook of the American Indian: Southwest*. 9. (Washington, DC: Smithsonian Institution, 1979).

The Talayesva quotations are from *American Indian Prose and Poetry: The Winged Serpent*, Margot Astrov, ed. (New York: Capricorn Books, 1962 reprint).

The quote from Koianimptiwa's song is from *The Indians' Book: Songs and Legends of the American Indians*, Natalie Curtis, ed. (New York: Dover Publications, 1968 reprint).

Text copyright © 1995 by Virginia Driving Hawk Sneve
Illustrations copyright © 1995 by Ronald Himler
All rights reserved
Printed in the United States of America
First Edition

Library of Congress Cataloging-in-Publication Data
Sneve, Virginia Driving Hawk.
The Hopis / by Virginia Driving Hawk Sneve ; illustrated by
Ronald Himler. — 1st ed.
p.   cm. — (A First Americans book)
Includes index.
ISBN 0-8234-1194-X (hardcover : acid-free paper)
1. Hopi Indians — History — Juvenile literature.   2. Hopi Indians —
Social life and customs — Juvenile literature.   [1. Hopi Indians.
2. Indians of North America.]   I. Himler, Ronald.   II. Title.
III. Series: Sneve, Virginia Driving Hawk.   First Americans book.
E99.H7S63   1995   95-1259   CIP   AC
973'.04974 — dc20

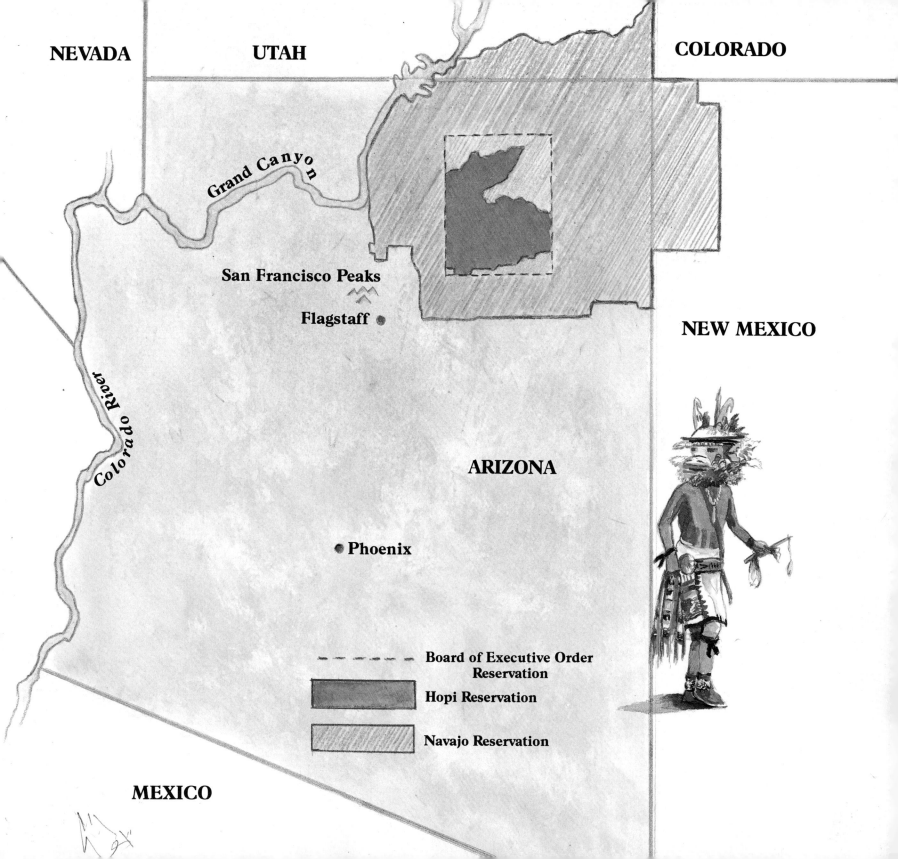

NEVADA

UTAH

COLORADO

Grand Canyon

San Francisco Peaks

Flagstaff

Colorado River

NEW MEXICO

ARIZONA

Phoenix

Board of Executive Order
Reservation

Hopi Reservation

Navajo Reservation

MEXICO

CREATION

I realize that there have been many before me who have taken the same steps and have made the same search — and have seen the same beauty.
AL QOYAWAYMA

**Kokyang Wuqti
(Spider Woman
kachina)**

Long ago, Tawa, the Sky God, and Grandmother Spider created the earth. Grandmother Spider, all of the animals, and the people lived in the dark underworld. Tawa told Grandmother Spider to put all things in order. She began by dividing the people into many nations and giving them names. She divided the animals and gave them names, too. Now all creatures knew who they were.

Grandmother Spider and two grandsons, the Hero Twins, led the animals and the people out of the dark land. They climbed a pine tree, moving up to a dimly lit world. Grandmother Spider led them on. As they climbed, it got lighter. At last they emerged from a hole in the floor of a canyon. They stepped out into brightness on the surface of the earth.

Grandmother Spider sent the animals and nations of people to live in different places on the earth. She separated the Hopi nation into clans, with one animal to lead each one. The clan was named for the animal that headed it.

Spirits, called Kachinas, came to help the Hopi clans. They taught the Hopis how to work together to plant crops, irrigate the soil, hunt, gather firewood, keep the village clean, and perform the special ceremonies that would keep them in touch with the spirits.

In this creation story, the first humans to emerge from the underworld became the Hopis.

MESAS

We are all in there, every living thing.
DEXTRA QUOTSKUYVA

Hopi village on top of mesa

The name Hopi is short for *Hopituh Shi-nu-mu*, which means "the peaceful people."
The Hopis avoided fighting unless they had to defend themselves.

Until about the mid-thirteenth century, the Hopi communities were scattered over the
desert. Only a few were on high hills. The Navajos, Apaches, and Utes attacked the Hopis
on the low ground. Gradually, more of the Hopis moved to three flat-topped hills. They
are the southern prongs of Black Mesa in what is now Arizona. From east to west the
hills were named First Mesa, Second Mesa, and Third Mesa. The three mesas can be
seen from each other. The word "mesa" means "table" in Spanish.

The Hopis are related to the western or desert Pueblos. Like the Pueblos, each village managed its affairs through its spiritual leaders. There was no single leader for all of the Hopi villages.

In the past, Hopi villages may have housed about two hundred people. Rooms were added in steps, with the higher steps set back so that the roofs of the rooms below could be used as balconies.

Several relatives and their families may have shared a household: the mother and father, adult married sisters, their husbands and children, unmarried brothers, and often a grandmother. They either all lived in the same house or in additions or buildings close by.

COAL, BASKETS, AND POTTERY

*I know that some of this clay may even contain
the dust of my ancestors.*
AL QOYAWAYMA

**Walpi pottery,
1860–1900**

basket, 1930

The Hopis mined coal from prehistoric times up through the seventeenth century. Both surface and underground mining were done. They used the coal to heat their houses and kivas, or sacred meeting places, and burned it during rituals. They used the ash heaps to fire their pottery.

For the last six centuries the Hopis have made fine baskets for carrying and storing food and other things. They have also made beautiful pottery for cooking, eating, and storage.

COMING OF THE WHITE MEN

Humbleness means peace, honesty — all mean Hopi.
PERCY LOMAQUAHU

In 1540 the Spanish came to the Southwest to explore and look for gold. At first the Hopis were afraid when they saw the white men. They told the explorers about the Grand Canyon and led the Spanish to its rim.

Jesuit missionaries tried to convert the Indians. They forced the Hopis to worship the white men's god and work as slaves. The Hopis resented the white men who forbade them to practice their traditional ceremonies. They hated being treated as slaves. That was why some of the Hopi villages joined in the Pueblo uprising of 1680. The Indians killed many Spanish and forced the rest to leave.

A Pueblo tribe, the Tewa, who had fought the Spanish, thought that the white men would return and kill them. They went to live with the Hopis. The Tewa built their village at Hano on First Mesa. They were a warrior tribe and were welcomed to the mesa.

The Spanish returned in 1692 and tried again to convert the Hopis. But the Hopis destroyed their churches and forced the missionaries to leave. Because the Spanish did not stay, the Hopis kept their traditional ways. However, they learned to use Spanish knives, axes, crowbars, and woodworking tools. The Hopis caught cattle, horses, burros, and sheep which had strayed from the Spanish.

The Hopis tried to remain peaceful, but Mexicans, Apaches, and Navajos stole their crops and ruined their gardens. Hopi enemies also took Hopi captives to sell as slaves in Mexico.

FOOD

piñon cones and nuts

Mother corn nourished the Hopi people.
POLINGAYSI QOYAWAYMA

corn

squash

pumpkin

The Hopis were excellent farmers. Every village had its own land. Some farmland was as far as twenty to thirty miles from the mesa. Little rain falls in the Southwest, but the Hopis mastered "dry farming" by using what water they had. They learned how the water flowed after a rainstorm, and planted their crops in the path of floods. They built dams to hold water and knew how to irrigate their fields. Their mesa homes were near springs that provided drinking water.

The most important crop was corn. The Hopis raised blue corn but also grew squash, pumpkins, gourds, several kinds of beans, and cotton. After the Spanish arrived, the Hopis grew onions, chilies, and melons. They planted peach and apricot orchards, too.

In addition to growing their food, the Hopis gathered many kinds of roots, leaves, berries, nuts, and seeds. They harvested the piñon nut, a special favorite, in the early fall. They ate wild onions raw or added them to stew. The broad-leaved yucca was used as a sweetener. Yucca roots provided a kind of soap, and yucca fibers were made into cords and rope. Willow and sumac stems were made into baskets.

The Hopis ate wild game and learned to eat beef and mutton after they got cattle and sheep from the Spanish.

MEN

*I had learned a great lesson and now knew that the ceremonies
handed down by our fathers mean life and security.*

TALAYESVA

**throwing club
for hunting rabbits**

weaving spindle

The men were skilled hunters of ground squirrels, gophers, and rabbits. They surrounded rabbits and drove them to the center of the hunters' circle. They stunned the rabbits by throwing sticks at them. Then they killed them.

On rare occasions, the Hopi men formed hunting parties to travel into the Great Plains for buffalo. They drove the buffalo into canyons and shot them with bows and arrows.

The men and boys worked the fields, harvesting the corn and beans. They removed the beans from the pods by pounding them with a stick. The men cared for livestock, gathered wood, and wove cotton and wool into cloth. Clothing, moccasins, and drums were also made from animal hides. Bones were fashioned into tools, and sinews made bowstrings.

Men were and still are the leaders of secret societies. The members meet in the clan's kiva, an underground room shaped like a rectangle. It is a sacred place, and on certain days during the year, it is used for ceremonies. At other times, men use the kiva to visit, relax, or discuss important matters concerning the village.

Two to six kivas may be in a village. There is a sacred hole inside that stands for the opening from which the first humans emerged from the underworld. The main floor reminds the Hopis of the place where the humans came out of the darkness into dim light. A raised platform is a symbol for the humans moving up into brighter light. The kiva's long-poled ladder leads to the ceiling entrance and stands for the tree the first humans climbed to reach the present world.

inside the kiva

WOMEN

That's the way Grandmother Nampeyo taught me.
DAISY HOOEE

prayer stick

traditional manta

metate (stone dish) for grinding maize

wedding robe with reed suitcase

The Hopis trace their heritage through the mother's line, and marriage within the clan is forbidden. The clans are generally named for an animal, and the Hopis believe that the name helps to connect them to the animal's special powers.

When a woman married, her groom and his closest male relatives made her wedding robes, belt, and moccasins. The bride carried a reed "suitcase" in which another robe and belt were rolled. After the wedding, the groom moved into his wife's home. He continued to keep in touch with his mother's clan, but his children became members of his wife's clan.

A Clan Mother kept the prayer sticks and other items sacred to her clan. Members lived in houses built next to her home. Sections of land were set aside for different community groups, and individual fields were owned by women in the clan.

Women also owned the seeds for next year's planting, the springs, the cisterns, and small gardens. After the men harvested the crops, the women prepared the food and stored it in pots and baskets.

The women and girls spent much of their time preparing corn for eating. Although they boiled or roasted fresh ears, they dried most of the corn. They kept it until the next year's crop was harvested. The women and girls spent several hours a day grinding corn into meal.

making piki

The meal was boiled and made into a gruel, or baked into bread. A favorite was *piki*, delicate thin sheets made from a batter baked on a hot polished stone.

In addition to preparing food, the women cared for the children, made pottery and baskets, cleaned the house, and hauled water.

Men owned the orchards, but the ground beneath the trees belonged to the women. The men also made the women's *mantas*. The manta was a dress fastened over the left shoulder. A sash was tied around the waist.

CHILDREN

All the knowledge needs to be handed down because someday we'll be the old people.

TRACY KAVENA

When a Hopi baby was born, a perfect ear of white corn was placed next to the infant. The corn stood for Mother Earth. At the end of twenty days, a perfect ear of corn was rubbed over the baby to bless it in a naming ceremony. This ritual was repeated when the child was initiated into a clan society, and again when the child became an adult.

A Hopi baby stayed in a cradle basket or board for most of six months. After the child began to crawl, he or she was watched by an older sister. By the age of four years, boys and girls could go wherever they wanted in the village. They were part of all village activities. Young children often wore no clothing, but later dressed like the adults.

Girls went with their mothers to haul water, and boys did errands for their fathers. By age six, the boys began to help their fathers in the fields. They scared birds away from ripe fruit and kept prairie dogs out of the cornfields. Also at the age of six, a boy began to help his father's brothers. As a boy grew older, he ran errands, chopped wood, and learned to care for the sheep and cattle.

By age seven, boys began initiation into male ceremonies so that they could sing and dance in the kiva when they got older. Girls could also learn about the ceremonies, but they did not belong to any of the male societies that wore kachina masks.

After age six, girls were responsible for watching over the youngest or next-to-the-youngest child in their family. Older girls helped carry water, sweep the floor, tend gardens, shell corn, and cook. They also began to help with the daily task of grinding corn. By age twelve, girls were expected to stay at home. A girl never wandered about the village without being with an older woman. She could now become a member of a woman's society.

By age sixteen, both boys and girls were well trained to take on adult duties.

When girls were old enough to be married, their hair was fashioned into a "squash blossom." The hair was parted in the middle, and each side was wound in a figure eight around a bent willow frame. After marriage, the hair was worn in two plaits or braids.

By the time a young man was twenty-one, he had undergone more training for ceremonies. He was given a new name that he used for the rest of his life.

CEREMONY

Over your field of growing corn,
all day shall come the rushing rain.
FROM KOIANIMPTIWA'S SONG

kachina dancer

musical instrument

black ogre
kachina doll

The Hopis' religion cannot be separated from everyday life. The Hopis believe they have to take care of the earth and keep their ceremonies on behalf of all humans. The rituals represent the Hopis' way of life from birth until death. One or more secret societies perform a ceremony which represents a part of that way. The members of a society may belong to many clans. But the head offical is a member of the clan that owns the kiva where the ceremony takes place. Other dances are held in the outdoor plaza.

The Hopis' ceremonial year is divided into halves. The kachina season is from late December to mid-July. The Kachinas are the link between the Hopis and the natural forces that control the universe. The Hopis believe that the kachinas have taught men how to make masks and costumes for their rituals. Men with special training wear the kachina masks and participate in the ceremonies. The masks have the power to turn the men into the kachina spirits. The kachinas will bring rain to the dry desert so that the crops will grow.

Masked men guard ceremonies to keep away unwanted visitors. Sometimes they act as clowns. Other times, they bring kachina dolls to teach the girls about the spirits. They bring ball games or toy bows for the boys. Special kachinas visit naughty children to make them behave better.

After the ceremonies, the kachinas leave. They go to their home believed to be in the San Francisco Peaks, near what is now Flagstaff, Arizona.

sacred clowns at entrance to kiva

Summer ceremonies in mid-July are mainly for ripening crops. In August the Snake Dance is performed. By dancing with snakes, the Hopis honor the reptile whose form is like the lightning of a thunderstorm. At the end of the ceremony, the snakes are returned to the desert, carrying prayers for rain.

Summer is also the time that the Butterfly and other dances take place. Young men and women dance together.

In the fall, Hopi women's societies have a series of ceremonies to honor the ripe crops. They dance and throw presents to the onlookers.

In this snake dance, the dancers hold the snakes in their mouths. Each dancer has a helper who distracts the snake by brushing it with a wand. Sometimes, rattlesnakes are used.

RESERVATION

There's just no sense in forgetting what was there before.
DEXTRA QUOTSKUYVA

Fort Defiance

In 1848 northern Arizona and New Mexico became part of the United States. In 1849 the U.S. government assigned an agent to all of the Indians of the Southwest. In 1851 Fort Defiance was built to control the Navajos. Hopi leaders visited the fort to ask for military protection from the Navajos who were raiding, killing, and taking Hopis captive.

White explorers and tourists visited the fort, bringing smallpox with them. In 1853–54, it led to the death of hundreds of Hopis. In 1864 the first Hopi Indian agent was appointed. In the same year, a severe drought began that lasted for several years. A great number of Hopis starved. Another smallpox epidemic struck, killing more Hopis. It was many years before the Hopi mesas were again filled with people.

By 1874 the U.S. government had begun constructing an agency center at Keams Canyon. Again, the white men tried to get the Hopis to become Christians. They were not too successful. The Hopis believed that their traditional ceremonies gave them a secure way of life that was better than the white men's religion.

In 1882 the U.S. government set aside an area for the Hopi reservation. A government school was opened at Keams Canyon in 1887. From then until 1911, Hopi parents were forced to send their children to school. They knew that their traditional life would change when the children learned English and new ways. Some Hopi families fought this change and were even sent to prison. Eventually all of the mesas had schools and the Hopis' isolation was ended. Still, despite the changes that education brought to the Hopis, they have continued their ceremonial life.

school building, Keams Canyon

TODAY

*If the land is abused, the sacredness
of Hopi life will disappear.*
HOPI ELDERS

In 1924 the Hopi were included among the American Indian tribes declared U.S. citizens by Congress. But many Hopis continued to resist the white men's way. In 1935, under the U.S. Indian Reorganization Act, the Hopis formed a tribal council. Most Hopis were pleased with the idea of one council for all of the villages. The council ended in 1940, and it was not re-formed until 1951. Since that time the council has worked to get leases for prospecting, exploring, and drilling for oil, gas, and minerals. This has brought regular incomes into Hopi villages. In 1966 a joint-use area with the Navajos was leased to the Peabody Coal Company. The company began strip-mining an area of Black Mesa in 1970. Today, the company pumps billions of gallons of water from underneath Black Mesa for processing the coal for power plants.

Some of the Hopis fear that the runoff from the mining area harms their crops. They worry that the mining damages and pollutes land, water, and air. But others want the income from the leases and jobs with the coal company.

Over many years Hopi lands gradually came to be completely surrounded by the Navajo reservation. This has caused disagreements between the Navajos and Hopis. In 1937 the government ruled that the Hopi lands become smaller, and the remaining acres be shared with the Navajos. The Hopis were unhappy about losing so much land and asked the U.S. Indian Claims Commission for money for the land. In 1970 the commission ruled in favor of the Hopis, but no settlement was made.

Today many Hopis find jobs in non-Indian communities working as businessmen, teachers, nurses, and forest-fire fighters. Those Hopis who prefer to stay in their mesa homes still farm as their ancestors did, and some work at jobs near the mesas. Others earn money from carving, painting, and making baskets, jewelry, and pottery. Over the years each mesa has become known for a different craft. Third Mesa makes wicker baskets; Second Mesa creates coiled baskets. The villages of First Mesa are best known for their pottery. Hopi arts and crafts are famous all over the world.

Once only women made pottery, but today men are also potters.

The Hopi Cultural Center on Second Mesa opened in 1970. It includes a tribal museum, crafts shop, restaurant, and motel. Hopis can read of mesa activities in the *Hopi Tribal News*, a newspaper published at Kykotsmovi, Arizona, and they have built the Hopi High School.

The Hopis' traditional beliefs and ceremonies are known as the "Hopi Way." Even if Hopis live and work in cities far from the mesas, they go home for the ceremonies and continue to follow the Hopi Way.

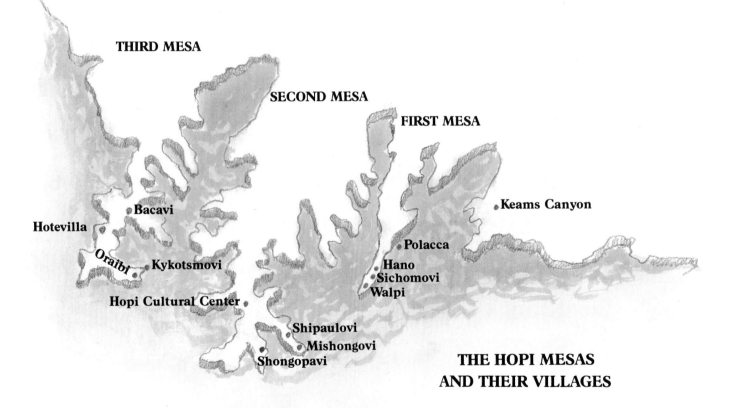

THIRD MESA

SECOND MESA

FIRST MESA

Keams Canyon

Bacavi

Hotevilla

Polacca

Oraibi   Kykotsmovi

Hano
Sichomovi
Walpi

Hopi Cultural Center

Shipaulovi

Mishongovi

Shongopavi

**THE HOPI MESAS
AND THEIR VILLAGES**

Corn is our mother —
and only the Cloud People can
send rain to make it grow.
They come from the six directions
to examine our hearts.
If they are good they gather above us
in cotton masks and white robes
and drop rain to quench our thirsts
and nourish our plants.
Keep bad thoughts behind you
and face the rising sun with
a cheerful spirit,
as did our ancestors in the days
of plenty.
Then rain fell on all the land.

TALAYESVA

"Learn from Me About the Rain Clouds" kachina

Index